SECOND-HAND DOG
How To Turn Yours Into a First-Rate Pet

HOW TO TURN YOURS
INTO A FIRST-RATE PET

by Carol Lea Benjamin

Illustrations by Author

First Edition

HOWELL
BOOK HOUSE
New York

Copyright information:
Parts of this book were previously published in a slightly different
form in *Pure-Bred Dogs/American Kennel Gazette* in August, 1980,
January, 1981, March and September, 1984, May and September,
1985 and February, March, August and October, 1987.

Howell Book House
Macmillan Publishing Company
866 Third Avenue, New York, NY 10022
Collier Macmillan Canada, Inc.

Library of Congress Cataloging-in-Publication Data

Benjamin, Carol Lea.
  Second-hand dog.

  Summary: Describes the care, training, and rehabilitation of previously owned or formerly homeless dogs, focusing on their special
problems and needs.
  1. Dogs--Training. 2. Dogs. [1. Dogs--Training]
I. Title.
SF431.B423 1988   636.7'0887   88-748
ISBN 0-87605-735-0

Macmillan books are available at special discounts for bulk purchases
for sales promotions, premiums, fund-raising, or educational use.
For details contact:

> Special Sales Director
> Macmillan Publishing Company
> 866 Third Avenue
> New York, NY 10022

10 9 8 7 6

Printed in the United States of America

For *Scarlet*, who is loyal,
 Lefty, who makes me laugh, and
 my sweetie, *Stephen*, who built a staircase the dogs could use to come up to the loft bed.
 I love you guys.

And for *Oliver*. Still missing you, Red.

Contents

Acknowledgements

THE AUTHOR wishes to thank *Pure-Bred Dogs/American Kennel Gazette* and its staff for support and feedback, as well as for allowing me an ongoing forum for opinions and ideas about dogs and their behavior. My appreciation, too, to Howell Book House for saying *yes* more often than *no* and especially to Elsworth Howell,who gave me that all-important, first *yes* when I had my first book idea.

My thanks to Captain Arthur Haggerty, *the* dog trainer. I've learned a lot from you, kid. I am grateful to Micky Niego, Coordinator of Companion Animal Services at the A.S.P.C.A., for enthusiastic support and friendship (Hi, Jake!) and to Maryann Akers-Hanson, prom queen and great, funny writer, *the b word*.

My gratitude to Mordecai Siegal and the Gaines Dog Research Center for their wonderful photographs. And for the use of your beautiful faces in our pictures, thank you,dogs and people.

With a hug and a kiss for Victoria Halboth, a *mensch* in anyone's book.

Introduction

WHETHER he was born in the bushes behind the laundromat or an adolescent abandoned to the streets by his once-upon-a-time owner, the streetwise stray can be a real challenge to incorporate into your life. The famous "he followed me home, can I keep him, Mom" canine is a special animal that needs time and space, calm and understanding.

This is a dog that has had to compete to stay alive; he's fought for food, scrambled for shelter. His reliance on his inborn canine savvy kept him alive long enough to meet up with you. Now you've taken him in and it becomes a crash course in Canine Socialization and Human Interaction 101.

If he's street-born, chances are he's never heard a toilet flush or seen a hair dryer in action. He gobbles up his food, throwing furtive glances left then right. The acoustics of the indoor environment make him anxious. Edgy, he whines and paces. A sudden sound and he's either bolt upright and ready for action or slithering along behind you.

Be reasonable in your expectations. Be sensitive. It's culture shock, pure and simple. Just imagine that you've been snatched away from home and suddenly find yourself in an aboriginal forest community. No language or gestures in common. Communication is by trial and error. Put yourself in his place. Then be patient and supportive. You'll succeed.

The stray who has been "previously owned" enters your home with a completely different set of baggage. Leashes, hands, rolled up newspapers and magazines, feet, chairs and sticks are just some of the pieces of training equipment that may have been used on this dog. Words like "come here" and "lay down" may bring forth a reaction other than the one you expected. This dog is the product of a never-ending series of miscommunications and surreal expectations.

As an adolescent or adult dog, he's already formed his opinion regarding humans. Be prepared to meet with confusion, reluctance and resistance as you retrain this fellow. He may flinch when you reach to pet him or when you make a sudden move or raise your voice. Don't let yourself be held hostage by thoughts of past cruelties and abuse. Don't treat him like a victim. The key here is confidence. Build his with firm consistent training and you'll turn him around.

The dog that you adopt from the shelter may be a rescued stray or a dog that someone has voluntarily surrendered for adoption. Somehow this pooch let someone down: too active, too noisy, too aggressive, too friendly. Or he's a victim of circumstance. An owner who died, is too ill or was arrested. He may have come to you because of a newborn who is allergic. Whatever, he's separated from those he loves and trusts. He waits for them to return, airscenting for the familiar smells that make him feel good all over. He misses them, he mourns them. His pack, his family . . . where are they?

When you get him home he's confused and disoriented. Sights and sound are simultaneously familiar and unfamiliar; things are jumbled up. He jumps on the couch and bed, he drinks from the toilet bowl, barks at the phone and makes wild lunges at strangers. In another life these behaviors may have been encouraged or maybe just not discouraged. Don't worry; he'll catch on. He'll get past it all. He'll become your dog.

Taking on the responsibility of a dog with a past is hard work. Make sure you and he are indeed suited for each other; that you can meet his needs for activity and companionship according to his breed type. Most of the problem behavior you'll encounter is an expression of the dog's inability to cope with the demands of your personality and lifestyle. Things may proceed slowly; you'll hit frustrating learning plateaus. But if you're committed you'll get there. Remember that the basic period of adjustment can be anywhere from six to twelve weeks. Go into this with your eyes open . . . and then stand back and marvel at the transformation. It will knock your socks off!

MICKY NIEGO
Coordinator of Companion Animal Services
A.S.P.C.A.
New York, N.Y.

Mordecai Siegal

14

1
Dimitri - A True Story of Survival and Spirit

EACH FALL when summer residents leave the country to go back home, each June when college students disappear rapidly after final exams, or simply when that darling Old English Sheepdog puppy bought on impulse in a pet shop shows his true colors (his adult size, his normal need for exercise, education, grooming and attention), dogs by the thousands are abandoned to fend for themselves like so many hairy hobos. Some wander around, growing more fearful by the day, until some mindless automobile puts them out of their misery. Some die slowly of disease or malnutrition. Unloved, uncared for, utterly abandoned, they forage in garbage cans and hunger for affection, a sad testimony to man's indifference to the needs of animals we have made dependent on us.

It is hard to believe, in a culture that worships the new and the shiny, that so tarnished and shopworn a specimen as a mistreated and abandoned dog could indeed become new and shiny again. But it can. This is the story of Dimitri.

Sometime during the last Thanksgiving holiday, Dimitri crossed the path of a young photographer and her artist husband. It was, one can now say, an incredible stroke of luck for the hapless Shepherd. How long he had been wandering the streets of Brooklyn and from whence he came is anyone's guess. On this night, when his fate changed radically, he was so ill that he was close to dying. Even externally, the picture was grim. The dog had a severe case of mange,

15

They forage in garbage cans and hunger for affection.

so severe that, save a few hairs on his head, he was bald. His raw skin was full of sores and what appeared to be "lash marks" lined his sides. Paul and Cindy didn't think long about the possible consequences of their action. They just could not leave the dog on the street.

For weeks, Paul and Cindy occupied themselves with the sick Shepherd. It took a couple of months of tender, loving care and good food before he had gained weight and was again covered with hair. The almost miraculous physical recovery had already taken place at the time I met Dimitri, but he was still fearful and anxiety was provoked by the slightest change of routine. Often he acted frightened or anxious for reasons we could not understand. Of course we knew we could never completely unravel the mystery of his gruesome past. But like any other creature, he carried it with him and sometimes, by his behavior, we could guess at some of the things that might have happened to him.

When I first saw Dimitri, he appeared to be very apprehensive. He didn't flinch when you neared him, though Paul reported that he used to. What struck me most were his eyes. Rather then being soft, shining, innocent and round, they were anxious, guarded and pinched looking. I suspected that there would be a dramatic change in his face as we worked with him and used training and affection to help restore his sense of worth, pride and dignity. At least, this was my fervent hope.

I let Dimitri take his time and come to me when he was ready to make friends. In the meantime, we talked about him and Cindy told me of the problems they were having. They were most concerned with his destructive rampages in the apartment. He would also urinate indoors at unpredictable intervals and when out on a walk, he'd pull so hard that Cindy had trouble managing him. Paul had taught him to sit and wait while he put his coat on to take Dimitri out and had begun to try to get him to heel. However, since the dog had been so ill and had such an awful history, Paul was reluctant to correct Dimitri and not sure when to follow up or be firm.

Dimitri was affectionate and not difficult to get to know. After an hour or so of intermittently petting Dimitri and taking a history from his owners, I felt it was time to see how Dimitri would react to training. I put his leash on him and asked him to sit and stay, indoors. When he broke the stay, I walked him back to the spot and repeated

17

the command. Within a few minutes, the first changes in his face were evident. He was, like most dogs, torn between fascination with "brain work" and a reluctance to give up control of his behavior. Unlike most dogs, here was an animal who had led a degrading existence. He had lost the feeling that simply because he was alive, he was terrific. Something in achieving the execution of a simple command stirred in him the feeling that he was really something, a *can-do* dog. And his feeling was visible. It was an exciting moment for Dimitri and for the three humans breathlessly watching him catch on and get hooked.

Now you are set up for a happy ending. Dimitri whips through the training course. An anonymous party mails us his papers. We brush his coat, get him into shape and run with him straight to Madison Square Garden for Westminster, right? Wrong! Now we have a dog who sits and stays and eats couches. Now we have a happy beginning. Patience, readers. Things always take four times as long as you guess.

Still on our first lesson, we decide to take Dimitri out. The problem with pulling is so severe that Cindy is having a hard time walking him. I don't feel it can wait. Also, the training will be one factor in helping the destructiveness problem. And, most important, Dimitri is hooked and happy and raring to go. Every now and then I see his eyes change, just for a second. When his curiosity is peaked, his eyes open wide and he has that round-eyed, innocent look we are all so mad for in our dogs. Paul tells me that Dimitri used to look up at him that way when he was trying to teach him to sit at the curb. He had noticed the profound difference in the dog's eyes whenever he was learning something new.

In a few minutes, with gentle leash corrections and a plain, leather collar (no choke chain), Dimitri is heeling. Moreover, his tail, which he often carries tucked under his belly when out of doors, is up and almost wagging. He is carrying his head higher, too. He is pleased. We are bursting. On this high we return to the apartment and plan the next lesson.

No dog learns in an entirely smooth fashion and, of course, Dimitri was no exception. I found him to be extremely bright and very excited by learning. He would get bored quickly and could best be educated by being intrigued. We had to go new routes, change our routine, work silently sometimes, teach lots of new material and keep surprising Dimitri to hold his interest. Each week he looked more robust, his coat thickened and darkened, his eyes regained more of an open and innocent appearance. But the destructiveness faded slowly and caused much frustration. I suggested confining him, particularly after a rampage. Cindy and Paul were understandably reluctant to punish Dimitri in any way; however, after some time, they did confine him after he had chewed and it did have a dramatic, helpful effect.

There was also the problem of Dimitri urinating indoors which seemed to be keyed to his relationship with the couple's older dog. Sam dominated Dimitri and the indoor urinating seemed to always follow their squabbles. Finally the couple rolled up their living room rug for a while to separate the dog from his "spot." This was done after the rug had been cleaned, sprinkled with white vinegar and even shampooed, all to no avail.

While problems were slow to depart, they got milder as training progressed. Often a dog with a bad history will be less flexible than a dog who has been raised in a loving, nourishing environnment. Such a dog will be slower to give up anxiety-provoked bad habits and will react more dramatically to even the smallest change of routine. While these factors caused frustration, Paul and Cindy never lost sight of the fact that Dimitri had come very far from where he was when they found him. They were always patient with him and always pleased with his progress.

Quite by accident one day, poor old Sam got caught in the act and Paul and Cindy reported to me in embarrassment that the wet spots on the rug were not Dimitri's doing. Sam, who is quite old, still enjoys life to the hilt but has small bouts of senility now and then. When out in the park, he wanders off sometimes and has to be watched. And, on occasion, he seems to forget himself on the oriental rug. With a younger dog, I would have suspected that Sam, as dominant male, was marking his territory to assert his top dog status with the presence of another male in the house. And while this may have been a part of the housebreaking mishaps, old age was surely the larger part. Sam was given an extra walk during the day to help alleviate the problem.

Dimitri not only suffered from being blamed, for a time, for Sam's mistakes, but he also suffered from his subordinate pack

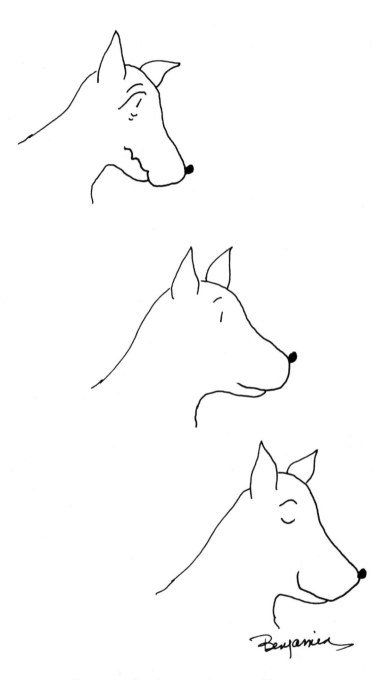

From apprehension to curiosity to self-esteem.

position. Sam, although old, still managed to tough out his leadership. Dimitri carried his pack position with him to the park. He was not aggressive with any of the other males and in fact, usually preferred to play with young dogs or females as a way of avoiding challenges and conflicts. This will probably change after Sam is gone. I have seen other cases where males of three or four or even five suddenly blossom when separated from a more dominant dog. But in addition to having another dog as "alpha" at home, Dimitri, who is about one year old at the time of this writing, seems to be having the puppyhood he missed while scrounging on the streets of Brooklyn trying to keep body and soul together. My guess is that his manhood will be late and slow in coming. I hope to be able to witness his emergence and flowering quietly from the sidelines as I have watched and enjoyed him become round eyed, strong of body, sparkling in appearance and able to enjoy both dogs and human beings once again.

Post Script: In the nicest way imaginable, Dimitri's story keeps weaving in and out of my own. It continues in the park where he and Sam play, where I take my dog to play, where all the neighborhood dogs congregate every evening to stretch their muscles, roll in the dirt, sniff, cavort, raise their hackles, break their commands, follow ancient rituals and have a grand, old time.

Last night, I stood quietly and watched my former student play with others of his kind. He looked strong and happy, the look of anxiety gone from his lovely, brown eyes. At one point, he recognized me and left the group of dogs to come close to where I was. Then softly he placed one paw on my waist and nuzzled my face before returning to his friends.

When I was ready to leave the park, I took a final glance at the group of playing dogs. The Borzoi, the Husky and the small, brown Terrier type, all of whom had been abandoned and then rescued at around the same time Dimitri was found, were still hard at play. They, too, like Dimitri, three seasons later, were enjoying life and thriving in loving, responsible homes. It is the hope, I suspect, of those who abandon dogs, that others will be moved to take them in. It is their hope, if they think about it at all, that the animal they callously turn their backs on will fill the needs of other humans, people like Paul and Cindy who could not leave an unappealing, damaged wretch of a dog to continue searching for something nameless he might never find.

Though most abandoned dogs are not as lucky as Dimitri, it is refreshing and encouraging to know that a dog *can* be successfully rescued and rehabilitated, that his sense of self can be restored along with his health and beauty, that his mind can be worked with after months of neglect, that he can become a happy, balanced pet. Though neglected and abused, Dimitri never became mean or aggressive. It is easy at this point to feel optimistic and gratified, seeing that the canine spirit is vigorous enough to survive such miserable treatment and still be there to respond to kindness and contact from loving humans.

Dimitri's story was first published, in a slightly different form, in *Pure-Bred Dogs/American Kennel Gazette*, official magazine of The American Kennel Club, in August, 1980.

It is because of Dimitri, and all those like him, that I wrote this book.

CAROL LEA BENJAMIN
New York City, 1987

2

Your Second-Hand Dog

D ID YOU FALL IN LOVE at the local animal shelter? There he was. His family moved away. Or he got too big. Perhaps he ate the arm of the couch or she had an unwanted litter. You saw potential there. You took him home.

Or you found him through an ad in the local paper. "Free to good home," it said. "Child allergic," it said, or "needs fenced yard."

He might even be a pure-bred dog, the one they had high hopes for and hung onto. But he was disappointing as a show prospect. Now he's six months old. He's not housebroken and he's more than a little shy. Sure he's got problems. Who doesn't?

Did you simply find him, wandering, hungry, with nowhere to go? With a little coaxing, he followed you home. You were sure you could find *someone* to care for him, to see the value in this tattered treasure. And so you did. And it was you.

In our throw-away culture, the second-hand dog has become commonplace. Your heart goes out to one. With love and work, you make him part of your family.

In order to become a terrific pet, your second-hand dog will need more of everything at first:

an extra dose of R and R (Rules and Regulations), more good food, more grooming, more contact, more company, more bonding activities, more long, solitary walks with you, more exposure to your particular environment, more exercise, more rides in your car, more games, more patient training, more room to be himself.

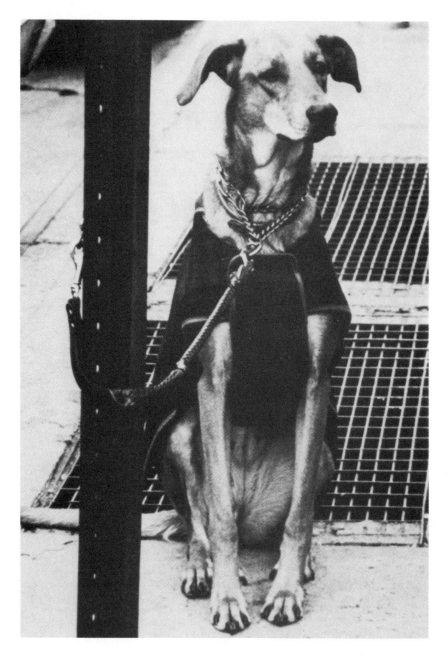

Mordecai Siegal

You've got your work cut out for you. But there'll be rewards, too — unqualified love, loyalty, companionship, someone to greet you when you come home, someone to make you laugh, to keep you feeling young, someone to get you out or keep you happy to stay in, someone who will place you above all others for as long as he shall live.

And there'll be help. Following, some information and some guidelines to assist you in your work.

Carol Lea Benjamin

3

How Dogs Learn — A Logical Place to Begin

"A little learning is a dangerous thing."
Alexander Pope

WHETHER OR NOT you're going to train him, your dog is going to learn a lot. Perhaps he already knows what the sound of the can opener means? Hasn't he learned how to sneak into your bed without waking you? Who's most likely to drop food onto the floor during and between meals? Your dog knows. He's got a brain and he uses it. He knows a lot more than you think he does.

Since he's always learning anyway, no matter his age, don't you want to monitor what he learns? You can help him to learn positive, useful things. You can avoid potential troubles as you go along. Understanding the many ways in which Fido learns, and using this information for mutual advantage, can give you an edge — a brighter, better-behaved dog with which to live.

How Fido Learns

1. Rewards and Punishments:

Give the dog a command, he obeys it, tell him he's terrific, repeat several times, he learns.

Find the spot, get the dog, tell him he's a gangster, show him where to spot next time, praise him, repeat when necessary, he's housebroken.

In short, reward a dog, or let him reward himself (think stolen roast beef), and he will repeat the behavior. Punish or correct a dog, and, with a little bit of luck, the behavior will be dropped. It's the old way of dog training. It still works.

Reward and punishment is one of the methods your dog's mother used to teach him. Starting from the moment he was born, she petted him with her smooth tongue when he was good and growled at him when he was naughty or in danger. Naturally, this is education any dog can understand.

2. Repetition:

Say the magic word, *sit*, for example, and put the dog in that position, eventually he'll do it on his own. Ask him to sit while you make his supper, soon enough he'll do it every day. Before you know it, he'll sit when he's hungry — even when you're nowhere near his dish. Habits are easy to create in dogs. His mother knew this, too. Time and time again, when he was small, she taught each important lesson, until, finally, he had learned.

3. Example:

Example is a great teacher. It's how you and I learned to talk. His mother taught him by her sterling example. She showed him, by example, when to be alert and when to be calm, whom to trust and whom to fear, when to explore and when to stay close to home. She showed him what a top dog was. She showed him how to be a dog. Not a puppy — a dog. And he filed it all away for when he was old enough — just as you did when you watched Mommy do the dishes while Daddy read the paper. (That's why you're in trouble now!)

And his litter mates taught him how to be a puppy — by reward and punishment as well as by example. (Dogs are clever enough to combine methods.) He'll copy your example, too, loving his education if you do, hating it if you feel training is cruel.

28

Reward . . .

. . . and punish. It works!

4. Accident or Serendipity:

You call your dog to come. He has an itch. He scratches it. You wait. Never, ever will he come quickly again. Accident for you. Serendipity for him. Now he knows how to get out of work. A little learning *is* a dangerous thing.

He leans on a door. It opens. Now he can open doors. Serendipity.

He puts his paws on the hot stove. Once. Accident.

5. Insight:

You can see it in his eyes when you are training him. He puts two and two together. He makes connections. He gets ideas.

Sometimes he experiences insights on his own. A Doberman I know who hated to retrieve once got a bright idea. He ran for the dumbbell and kept right on going — right into the woods. When he returned, the dumbbell was nowhere to be found. Two and two make four.

He's non-verbal, so he learns from body language, voice and posture. He can feel your moods and draw conclusions. He's learning all the time. Understanding the many ways in which Fido learns, and using this information for mutual advantage, can give you an edge — a brighter, better-behaved dog with which to live. (Repetition — it works for humans, too!)

4

An Alpha Primer (Because You Must Be in Charge)

Since the very first days man and dog spent together, in some cold cave on some wild terrain, there was a mixed species pack and there was a leader. Dogs are pack animals by nature. They need appropriate pack structure and leadership in order to survive well.

When you bring a dog into your family, you must become not only his caretaker, but his leader as well. There's nothing on earth that makes a dog feel more secure than having a strong leader, a mother figure, if you will, an *alpha* dog to call the shots.

In fact, in raising and training your dog, *alpha* is what it's all about.

If your bad dog is nasty, too clever for his own good, marking the house with urine, running away when you call him to come, scratching an itch when you say *down*, breaking his stays, guarding his bowl, growling when you roll over onto him in your own bed, *alpha* is what it is all about.

If your good dog sit-stays in the elevator, listens to anyone who takes his leash, lets you take his food away, does tricks on eye contact alone, looks to you for direction and approval, understands *no* and *okay*, no matter what, comes when called even if he's off leash, out of doors and playing with another dog, *alpha* is what it's all about.

Mordecai Siegal

Alpha is what it is all about.

Professional trainers know that it is a waste of time to try to train a dog without first establishing themselves as alpha to the dog. Every dog needs a leader to listen to and adore. If he doesn't have one, he takes the role hmself. Then he's nasty, too clever for his own good, marking the house with urine, running away when you call him to come, scratching an itch when you say *down*, breaking stays, guarding his bowl, growling when you roll over onto him in your own bed. Having so much to do and so little time, just like you, professional trainers establish short cuts to becoming alpha to any dog they meet. They deliver their message with body language, behavior, an air of confidence. You can, too. Here's how.

1. Always praise your dog as if you own it. Put your hands firmly on your dog. Hug the dog. Pat him so that your hand gets warm from the contact. Do not praise in an offhand or timid way.

2. Praise warmly, well and quickly. Do not drag out your praising of a working dog. Do not fawn over the dog just because he did one sit-stay. As my first teacher used to say, "He wasn't *that* good."

3. Reprimand fairly and quickly, then forgive. When you put your hands on your dog, do it with confidence and authority. NO — hands on does not mean hitting. Hands on may mean a collar shake, a leash correction, a surprising assist into a sit or down. Do it quickly and with authority. Then when you've made the dog do exactly what you want — once — give him a hug. That's alpha.

4. Give permission. Give it for what he is about to do anyway as long as it is okay with you. This does not mean you say OK when you see your dog about to steal the evening roast. This means you do say OK when your dog is about to get into the car for a ride with you, eat the food in his bowl, go out with you for his afternoon constitutional. It means that in a subtle way you are teaching the dog to look to you for approval and permission instead of making decisions on his own. Remember — the better behaved the dog, the more freedom and fun he can have.

5. Deny permission. Monitor your dog's behavior. Teach him some manners. Even if you like him to walk on your couch and coffee table, (you know who you are!) he shouldn't behave that way in

Act like a top dog — benevolent, but alpha.

other people's homes. When you take him to the lake, he should wait for permission to swim. It may be too cold some days or there may be too many young children swimming. And he should come onto your bed only with permission, too. Remember, you are in charge.

6. *Do a sit-stay.* My own very laid-back way of becoming alpha in five to ten minutes is to put the dog on a sit-stay. If he's a wild animal and he doesn't know the meaning of the word *obedient*, all the better. When he breaks, and he will, I put him back. If he breaks 14 times, I put him back 14 times. At the end of a few minutes, the dog knows you're alpha. He knows that anyone who holds his leash can call the shots. And this is with no yelling, no hitting, no electronic stimulation, no leaving him in the kennel or garage for three days, no nothing. Just a sit-stay. Easy. Effective.

7. *Stand tall.* Use your voice to express your confidence. Act like a top dog — *benevolent, but alpha.* Tough, but loving. Capable of getting what you want, what's necessary for safety and sanity. Never jerky, show-offy, arbitrarily unfair, sadistic. Never! Can a dog understand what's fair and what isn't? You bet!

8. *Be a model to your dog.* The top dog behaves with dignity, surety, confidence, authority, intelligence. Be like his mother, comfortable in the alpha role. It can help a dog be calm. Comfort is contagious.

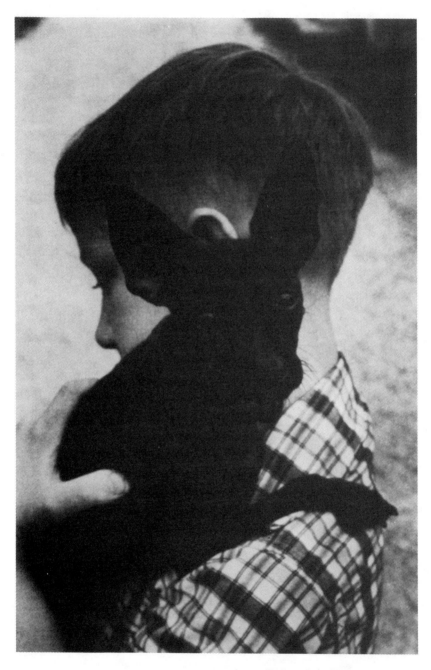

5
The Good Life —
What Your Dog Needs

I. He needs a crate - for housebreaking, problem prevention, and travel.

Give your wanderer a room with a view. Every dog needs a home of his own — a place to call his, a place that smells just right, a little den.

Every dog needs someplace to escape to. He needs a place to be put when he's young and learning the rules. He needs somewhere to be sent when he's been rotten and you can't stand the sight of him. Every dog needs a crate.

Your first job is to train the dog to accept the crate. In the beginning, always praise him when he enters his crate. Tell him he's a good dog when he comes out, too. Use the crate for only a few minutes the first few times and be sure to leave the door open. As a temporary measure only, to help your dog have positive feelings about his crate, feed him while he's in the crate. Praise him for eating in his crate. Let him leave whenever he's ready.

When he enters the crate easily, give him a rawhide bone to chew there and close the door. After a moment, open the door. If he comes out, fine. If he stays in the crate, fine.

Eventually, you will be able to close the crate door and stay in the room, going about your business. Then you will be able to feed, water and walk your dog, crate him and leave for an hour or so. At this point, after about a week, you should be able to slip into using the crate as and when you need it — as described next.

Do not leave your dog in his crate day and night. Do not put him in the crate without first walking him so that he can relieve himself and use up some of his boundless energy. Give him a chew toy and, when he's shown he can keep his crate clean and dry, give him a washable mat or towel to sleep on. Used wisely and sparingly, the crate can be your second best friend.

How should you use it? Let me count the ways:

1. Use a crate for housebreaking.

The crate is the best tool available and the only method that is guaranteed to get the job done no matter the age of the dog. Make a humane schedule — out every three hours for very young puppies, out every five to seven hours for adult, unhousebroken dogs. Feed, water and walk the dog. If the walk is successful, let the dog stay out of the crate but with you for a period of time you're sure he can remain clean in the house — fifteen minutes for beginning puppies, an hour for adult dogs, anywhere in between *that works* for dogs in the process of getting trained. After "play time," crate the dog until the next walk. When you take him out of the crate, take him right outside, on leash. Walk him. Watch him. Praise him when he does what he's there for. And continue as above.

If your dog is getting housebroken and you are giving him more freedom, what do you do when he goofs? Simple. Go back to day one. Start again. It simply means you went too fast. Slow is fast in dog training. Slow gets the job done for real.

What if your dog wets only at night? Crate him only at night. What if when he's crated, he lifts his leg and urinates out of the crate? Do four things: give him much more exercise, obedience train him, make absolutely sure you're alpha and switch from a wire crate to an airline crate. If he's going to urinate in his crate, he's going to have to sit in it until you get home and clean up. That will break the habit.

What if he soils his crate? If this happens more than for the first couple of days you are crate training, something is wrong. Is the crate the right size, the length of the dog when he's lying down? Is the crate immaculate? If not, you are teaching your dog to be dirty. Clean the dog and the crate any time there is an accident. Are you taking him out often enough and for a long enough time? Are you giving too much water or feeding him too much or too often? Is he sick and

38

unable to control himself? With these questions answered, the problem should be solved.

As the dog gets trained, lengthen the time he is allowed out of the crate, but leave the crate open for him. Most dogs love their little dens and use them when they want to rest. Eventually, the dog can have run of the house, unattended, and will keep things clean. Be patient.

2. Use a crate for chewing prevention.

An untrained, anxious dog can ruin your house if let loose unattended. When you cannot monitor the dog, keeping him in the room with you, keeping an eye on him, use his crate. Crating him when you go out and crating him when he cannot be monitored can save you from expensive, heartbreaking, needless destruction. I wouldn't dream of raising any dog without a crate. And furthermore . . .

3. Use a crate for discipline.

What happens when you goof and "let" your dog sneak away and leave a mess or chew a pillow and you want to kill him? Take the dog to the scene of his infraction — the mess, the torn pillow, the stain. His own scent in the area reminds him of what he did. Now, act angry. If you feel angry or frustrated with your dog's progress, never take it out on him. This is dog training, not dog abuse. With self control, shake the dog by his collar, saying NO, NO, NO. Then march him to his crate. THAT'S ALL YOU HAVE TO DO. The message is clear: If you are going to be rotten, be rotten in your house.

Will he hate his crate? NO! When you were a little brat and your parents sent you to your room because they couldn't stand the sight of you, did you hate your room?

If you are fair when you punish a dog, and fair means clarity, fair means communication, fair means consistency, the dog will take the punishment with equanimity. He will learn. He will grow. He will go on. His spirit will not be broken. He will not stop loving you. He will not stop loving his crate.

In addition, the crate works magnificently as a disciplinary tool. Even though your dog uses the crate for his own purposes, as a place of privacy, his own room, he still understands that when he has been rotten, you have used the crate for isolation. He does not want to be isolated in his crate. He wants to sleep in it with the door open when *he* feels like it. The whole point of correction is to do something the dog doesn't like to get him to stop doing something you don't like. When you use the crate for discipline, he gets the message. And he reforms. Yet he will still go into his crate happily when he wants to sleep or chew or when you want him there to ride safely in the car or merely be out from under. He can discriminate, of course, between being asked to go into his crate nicely when he's been good and being sent (shoved?) in when he has just been corrected. He's no dummy.

4. Use the crate for traveling.

The crate will keep your dog safe in a car. You can roll down the windows, pay tolls, open doors, without the fear of losing your dog. In addition, when he's riding in a crate, he can't suddenly land on your lap — or head — while you are executing a hairpin turn at 60 m.p.h.

Traveling with a dog crate means you will be able to stay overnight in motels without fearing damage when you leave the dog and go out to dinner. Sometimes a crate will get you into a place that wouldn't usually allow dogs. So even if the open crate doesn't fit in your sedan, having the crate folded in the trunk is a great idea when you're staying away overnight.

Wherever you park your dog's crate, in your den or in a motel room in a strange city, from his point of view, the crate says "home." No dog should be without one.

NOTE WELL: A small minority of older dogs will not tolerate confinement. Something in your dog's past may eliminate the possibility of using a crate.

In most cases, the crate will offer security to the dog who badly needs just that. Some will do better with their crate in the hub of the house, the den or the kitchen. Others need a quiet place. Some like a good view and even some conversation while they rest. Others need a towel draped over the crate or the comfort of a semi-closed airline-type crate rather than the wire models. This can be discovered by trial and error. Before you give up on the idea of the crate, work patiently and slowly, as detailed in this chapter, to try to get the dog used to it. Convincing him that the crate is benign cannot be done with words. It must be demonstrated and done so repeatedly.

II. He needs to bond with you.

Make time for your new dog to become part of your life. Keep him with you when you cook, write letters, do the lawn. Take him in the car when you go for the newspaper or the Sunday morning rolls. Talk to him and tell him he's terrific. But give him quiet time with you, too. Dogs are not verbal animals. They need time to absorb the way things are in silence. They need time, they need contact, to become attached.

III. He needs your patience, affection and quiet firmness.

Your rules and regulations will help make the dog secure in his new home. But he has lost something profound. He'll need reasons to feel proud of himself again. You can give him those. Whenever he does something worthy, let him know it. Don't gush and stop the training. Coo to him like his mother used to and keep the work flowing. Work is the best medicine for anxious, insecure creatures. It even works for people in trouble.

IV. He needs a diet of dog food.

Your dog needs a sensible, well-balanced diet of food made especially for his species — dog food. Read my lips. He does not need shrimp in lobster sauce, chocolate chip cookies with M&M's baked into them (You know who you are!), beer or French fries. He needs at least ninety per cent of his diet (See! I allow for a *little* pizza and an occasional ice cream cone.) to be a nutritionally complete, dry dog food, "flavored" *if it pleases you* with a few spoons of canned dog food or with a homemade chicken or beef broth. Most dogs, especially large dogs, do better on two meals a day. Simply divide the ration the dog food bag tells you is right for your size dog and feed half in the morning and half in the evening. Or, if you prefer, give your dog one main meal of dog food per day and one small "meal" of dog biscuits. Do not allow your dog to exercise vigorously immediately before or for a couple of hours after a big meal. Use common sense in adjusting his food intake according to his activity and the season. (Many dogs will drop a few pounds in warm weather and put on a little protective fat in the winter.) Make sure your dog has plenty of fresh water. Be sure, too, when you do give him an occasional treat of chicken or steak that you remove the bones. If

He needs a sensible diet — of dog food.

A silent reminder of who's who and what's what.

you have any questions about nutrition, vitamins, proper weight or other related concerns, ask your veterinarian for advice.

V. Groom him for mutual relaxation.

If your dog is kept clean and fresh and free of parasites and tangles, he'll feel better and look better. When his coat is clean and healthy, you'll pet him more often. More than that, as if that weren't enough, when you brush your dog, it will relax both of you. Studies show that contact with animals has a relaxing effect on both the human and the animal. You can't ask for more than that for simply brushing your dog and bathing him about once a month. My Shepherd, by the way, will get into the shower with me. I wet her down with the moveable, hand spray, soap her well with dog shampoo, rinse her off, blot her dry, let her out and clean myself. It's a quick and easy way to clean a cooperative dog.

VI. He needs quiet time.

The dog is not a verbal animal. (Anything worth saying once, my mother used to say, is worth saying twice. And she did, too.) He needs time to be a dog, to sniff, to swim, to roll on his back in the grass on a sunny day, to dig to China on the beach, to lie around and watch the sun go down. He needs some time alone, and some with you. And isn't a little quiet time just what your life is missing?

VII. He needs your company, so let him sleep in your room.

You can give your dog a free eight hours of your time by letting him sleep in your room. You keep him clean, don't you? And he's housebroken now, isn't he? And he's lonely sometimes, isn't he? He loves your quiet company. He's a pack animal, remember? And if it pleases you, and if he's not aggressive, sure, he can sleep on your bed. But do take the time to teach him OFF and let him up by invitation. A pat on the bed will get him there lickety split.

VIII. He needs appropriate eye contact.

Among wolves and wild dogs, direct eye contact is a threat. Only the alpha animal may use it. This he (or she) does, often.

In the wild, eye contact is used to keep the pack in line. It maintains order, it helps avoid conflict, it is a speedy, silent reminder of who's who and what's what. It is an important means of communication, though by no means the only one.

In our world, between human and dog, eye contact has a less rigid definition. Our pet dogs learn that eye contact can be loving and gentle. They learn that they can read a variety of messages via the eye, instructions, feelings, cues of all kinds. And they see, of course, that the old ways can still hold true, that the message *alpha* still comes from the eye.

Understanding the importance of eye contact, and lack of it, in dogs can help you to use this natural means of communication more effectively as well as more carefully. Here are some things you ought to know about eye contact in dogs:

1. Your dog is always reading messages from your eyes, whether or not you are consciously sending them. When your lips say *no, no* and your eyes say *yes, yes*, well, you know that routine.

2. He who initiates eye contact is usually sending the message that he is boss. (A word to the wise is sufficient.)

3. He who breaks eye contact first loses.

An informal record of 25 minutes was set by my Shepherd, Scarlet, and my daughter's Sheltie, Deela. At that point, I got tired of watching and left. If not for the fact that Dee had to go home, they'd still be there, eyes locked. But then again, herding dogs are prone to staring down other animals, aren't they? And aren't we animals, too?

My little dog, Lefty, stares at me when I read, knit or watch T.V. For months, I didn't pay attention. When I thought about it, I thought it was amusing. Then one day I realized what it was. He was staring. I was averting my eyes. Never mind that I was reading, knitting or watching T.V. To Lefty, as to any very alpha breed, I was averting my eyes. Every second that he sat there staring, he was winning, the little devil. Once I caught on, I simply turned my face to him and made eye contact. No, not the loving, tender kind. The kind that whistles as it cuts the air. Immediately, he looked away. A moment later, I saw the curl of his tail disappearing out of the room. Secure in my position, I went back to my book.

4. If a dog will not give you his eyes, he may be very submissive. You can work with your dog patiently and let him know that he can indeed make loving eye contact with you. Praise him when he does. Eventually, those furtive glances will become long, loving stares.

44

5. If a dog will not give you his eyes, he may be very dominant. He knows full well that to give his eyes to your more dominant ones would be to give in, to give up. Sure, he'll sit-stay for you. You have the leash, don't you? But he'll do it without looking at you and the looking, in this case, is what shows his recognition that you are boss and you call the shots. When on command, he should look to see what you want next. If he won't look, you've got your work cut out for you. For no matter how long he sits there, he's not a trained dog until he's willing to look submissively into your dominant eyes.

6. Is your dog of a breed that's not so hot off leash? I could name them all, but space won't permit. If you have any hope of training your dog to come or even listen when he's in the great outdoors, on leash, please, start by getting eye contact. Once or twice in a twenty-minute walk, call his name, the name only, and get him to look at you. Praise. Tell him OK and go on with your walk. Practice this until he does it affably. But don't badger him with it.

If he won't turn and look the first time you try, find a way to get him to do just that — whistle, take along a squeak toy, clap your hands (with the leash loop on your wrist for the moment). Once your dog will make eye contact, you have a shot at getting obedience. Without it, don't waste your time or his.

7. Use eye contact to warn. The wolves do. First of all, the more you use it, the more your dog gets in the habit of looking *to* you (rather than *at* you). He looks to you for direction. Give it to him. When he's about to raid the wastebasket, warn him with harsh eye contact. (Yes, of course you can make a noise to get him to look at you. But don't use his name when you are making a correction, even if it is a silent but deadly stare.)

8. Use eye contact to direct. I am going left, or right. The ball is there. The cookie is here. You'll faint when you see how well your dog can read these signals.

9. Use eye contact to praise. Send your warmth, approval and your love, eye to eye. It works. And it wouldn't break your face to add a smile. Dogs read those, too.

10. Use eye contact to start an action. My Golden Retriever barked on eye contact. So when I caught his eye and said, "Oliver, how old am I?" he went on and on. And on.

11. Use a break in eye contact to stop an action. When I broke eye contact with Ollie, he shut up — at 39, as if I were Jack Benny!

So then you can do, "What's the square root of 25?" And after the fifth bark, immediately after it, break eye contact. The eyes are tricky, too.

When it comes to understanding your dog and communicating your wishes to him, the eyes have it. When it comes to teaching dog obedience, which is almost what we are ready to do, there's nothing quite so powerful as keeping your dog emotionally attached to you via the eye. So here's looking at you, kid.

IX. He needs to be socialized — again and again.

Proper socializing insures a well-balanced, flexible animal who can take all kinds of surprises in his stride. It results in the dog who is able to accompany you out for the Sunday paper, the dog who is trustworthy with children, the dog from whom you can take a bone, the dog to whom you can offer a lasting place in your home and in your heart.

Following are some traditional and not so traditional ways to prepare your dog for any stress and for any joy that may come his way.

1. Let him be handled. A dog should be able to be handled by humans of all ages and both sexes. The way to teach him to accept this with equanimity is to begin having him handled by many types of people from the day of his arrival. When you adopt an older puppy or dog, this socializing process has already been done or not done. Still, you can go forward from where you are. When you take him out of doors, encourage nice people to handle him and encourage him to be affable and friendly. No, this will not destroy his ability to protect you should the need arise and should he be of that bent. Dogs distinguish very nicely between the good and the bad humans that they meet.

Give your dog lots of pleasant, social experiences which will help him to move from being secure at your side to feeling great and confident in the great big world. Gradually, he will learn to feel comfortable making new friends both at home and away — on the sidewalk outside your house, down the block, at the veterinarian's office, outside the shops in your town, village or city, in the lobby of your apartment building, in the park, visiting friends, on vacation at the beach or in the mountains. Let him know that people can be wonderful.

2. Let him not be handled. You don't always have to let people touch your dog. You don't have to let all people touch him, either. There are times when you will not want him handled — he's tired, you're in a hurry, you're tired, he's in a hurry, you're training him, he's busy sniffing, he needs to relieve himself, you simply are not in the mood. Perhaps he's great looking — or wearing a bow — and he's been over-handled already that day. Or you don't like the looks of the potential petter. Or he doesn't, and you trust him. You have the right not to amuse the world with your dog, too. He has the right to go about his business unmolested at times. Most people feel downright mean saying no when someone wants to pet their dog. Don't. Feel intelligent and protective. If you don't protect your dog, who will?

3. Housebreak your dog. If you want to be able to take him anywhere you are welcome, he's got to be housebroken first. Simple instructions are in the section on crates.

Once the job is done, make sure your dog is flexible in his habits. Make sure he can use dirt, grass, gravel, sand, pavement, sawdust, etc. so you can really take him anywhere. You can use a shortcut if you like, a phrase such as "Hurry up," or a gimmick such as walking him in a small circle, either of which will communicate rapidly to him in a new setting what the outing is all about. You'd be surprised how many dogs get stuck relieving themselves on one kind of surface or even in one spot and then get homebound. Not our sweetheart!

4. Get him used to other people's dogs. He needs you, for sure. He needs your love and friendship, your approval, too. But he also needs friends of his own kind — dog friends. He must learn to feel at least comfortable and at most wonderfully friendly with the other dogs in your neighborhood. If there's a park where dogs play, take him. If your neighbor has a nice, friendly dog, make a play date for your dog. There's nothing on earth that will please or tire your dog like play with one of his own.

5. Make him flexible. At least once a week, let your dog try something new — a visit to a friend's house (He's housebroken, isn't he?), on an overnight jaunt with you, an overnight stay at someone

Surprise him with lunch at the beach.

else's house, lunch at the beach, a visit to some kids or to a local nursing home. Let someone else walk him, feed him, brush him. Shake up the order of things. Let him explore your attic or your basement. Take him to a bookstore. Hike with him to a new environment. Take him swimming. Buy him an ice cream cone. Refresh him, challenge him, mature him with new situations, some pleasurable, some not. If he has trouble, help him through. Don't let him do an escape act. Be demanding. Praise him when he's brave and tries new things. Encourage him to be curious, investigative, bold. Learning how to cope will stand him in good stead for the rest of his life.

6. Make him rigid. In order for you to make him flexible, well-socialized and able to be blasé in all situations, he must learn to be rigid, too, about certain things. His housebreaking must be rigid — rigidly followed and rigidly enforced. His obedience must be rigid. He must always listen to you. He must always behave in an acceptable manner on outings. This does not mean he will behave like a little robot at home or when you play with him in the park. But the dog who is rigid in his behavior and manners can be taken everywhere. Thus, you will be able to get him used to noise, dogs, crowds, cameras, applause, fame and fortune. The dog who breaks his housetraining "just once in a while," or who jumps on strangers "sometimes" cannot go into stores for crowd training nor will he have all the pleasures he'd get were he a well-trained, well-seasoned pet.

7. Make him attractive so that people will be drawn to him, will play with him, will admire him. Keep him sparkling clean and well-brushed. Give him plenty of exercise for stamina. Put a gigantic bow on his collar. This works wonders in helping you to socialize a scary-looking breed. And for any breed, a bow on the collar is a way of attracting people to your dog, thus helping in the socialization process.

8. Teach him a trick or two. When you want everyone to love your dog so that your dog loves everyone, go for the laughs. Laughter makes any meeting easier. Laughter hands you and your dog the world on a silver platter. Choose something appropriate for your dog's size, shape and age, but do not worry about your dog's sense of dignity. I never met a dog who didn't love to make people laugh.

50

9. Make him confident with lots of positive reinforcement. When your dog does something right — swims for the first time, plays with a new dog, works well on a busy, crowded street, takes his first elevator ride, your praise and pleasure will build his confidence, making him feel both accomplished and terrific.

10. Give your dog the rich life — a wide variety of experiences, most of them *away from home*, so that he will be able to face with equanimity anything that might come his way. When my Golden Retriever, Oliver, met a chimp on roller skates at Bloomingdales, he wagged his tail. When the chimp took hold of his leash and began to skate down the aisle, Oliver heeled along at his side. That's equanimity! That's the kind of fun you can have with a well-socialized dog, a dog who's your sidekick, your buddy and, above all, the very best dog he can be.

X. He probably should be neutered.

Simply stated, there are more dogs in the world than there are people to care for them. The only reason to breed a dog is to improve a specific breed by using a recognized, outstanding example of that breed as "stock," or to fill a special need, i.e. dogs to lead the blind or aid the deaf. Neutered, your dog will be more tractable, less aggressive, less likely to break loose and run away, less apt to lift his leg indoors, friendlier to other dogs, unable to add to the over-population problem we now face. Please be responsible. Discuss neutering with your veterinarian.

XI. He needs to be protected.

Some folks won't walk a dog. They just open the door and let him out. He needs to run free, they say. I can't stand to see a dog confined, they claim. Then, when the dog gets hit by a car, or lost, or shot chasing deer, they shake their heads. Stupid dog, they say. You've heard them. Got himself run over, they mumble. They take no blame.

Your dog should never be allowed to "run free." Certainly, if he comes when called, reliably, and if you are with him, and if it's legal to have him off leash, take off the leash and let him run around in the park. But never let him out of sight. He might get lost. Or hurt. Or get into a fight. Or get hit by a car. Not this dog. Right?

Be sure you protect your dog in every way you can. He relies on you. You're all he's got. Take him to the veterinarian for a yearly check-up and inoculations. Diseases are more easily prevented than cured. Make sure he's got a license and even an identifying tattoo. Unlike a collar with a tag, a tattoo won't fall off. Protect your dog from people who tease or abuse dogs. Protect him from the heat and the cold. He's your charge. Keep him safe and well. He'll love you forever for it.

And finally, what we all need,

XII. A TRAINER'S TIPS TO PREVENT BITING

Don't let *your* dog bite the hand that feeds him — or any other hand, for that matter. Biting prevention should start the day you get your dog and continue for all his life. When working with your dog, be aware that when you correct an older dog for biting, he may get more aggressive before he gets less so. He may, in other words, defend his imagined position as top dog. So be sure you can handle the job before you take it on. If you feel you can't and you love your dog, hire a professional dog trainer to help you. When working with a trainer or on your own, be prepared to protect yourself. Work with a leash so you have some way of holding onto the dog and of correcting him. Keep water handy — a pot full, a bucket, a hose, even a water gun. A well-timed face full of water or shot of lemon juice can sometimes stop a bite from happening. And most important, when correcting biting, YOU MUST END UP THE WINNER EVERY TIME. If you back down, your dog will know it and that will make his aggression stronger. He's a pack animal, isn't he? Now, here are the rules to live by:

1. Nip nipping in the bud. Nipping is the forerunner of biting if it is allowed to go unchecked. Sure, your puppy is teething and he needs to chew. But even if his "love bites" are no problem when he's small, he's growing, isn't he? If he has the idea that human flesh belongs in his mouth, he's learning a bad lesson. As he gets older, he'll be more aggressive, a natural part of growing up. He'll play harder and harder, and he'll bite harder and harder.

When he nips, try a firm NO. If this doesn't stop him, grasp his collar by slipping your hand under it *or* snap on the leash and jerk him from side to side (this is how his mother, her mouth on his neck, might have corrected him when he was younger), repeating your angry NO. If he continues to nip, march him to his crate and leave him there to cool off. The message is: I won't play with you if you bite.

2. Be a smart cookie — use a leash. The leash is your training equipment and should be respected by your dog. So never let him chew it or tug it. When you are trying to correct biting, you must consider your own protection. Correcting with a leash, a jerk and release accompanied by the word NO or a shake from side to side, similar in feeling to what his mother did when he was naughty, is safer than attempting to correct the dog without equipment.

3. Newspapers are for reading. Never hit your naughty dog with a rolled-up newspaper. A cylindrical object swinging toward a dog is much more likely to increase aggression than to prevent it. If ever you must slap your dog, use your hand. But remember, a leash correction is safer and communicates well.

4. Teach your dog the command "Enough." NO means: What you are doing is wrong and you must never do it again. ENOUGH means: What you are doing is OK, but for now I want you to stop. Too complicated for a dog? Hardly. Most learn by tone of voice. Use NO for nipping, biting, growling. Use ENOUGH for wildness, excessive barking, roughness. It is an excellent tool in biting prevention.

5. Don't play rough, play active. Now hear this: BEHIND ALMOST EVERY BITING DOG IS A WELL-MEANING OWNER WHO ROUGHHOUSES WITH THAT DOG. Play active — toss a ball for your dog to retrieve, jog, race, bike with your dog, swim with your dog, teach him frisbee, toss a stick, let him race back and forth between two, three or four family members. NEVER, NEVER let your dog tug on clothing, bite on your arm, bite on your arm wrapped in a towel or a shirt, pull and tug on a towel or rope. NEVER, NEVER let your dog bite or pull his leash. NEVER, NEVER let him bite an object and swing in the air. Don't swing your hands in his face. This kind of teasing would make YOU want to bite. And above all, don't think that biting games will make your dog a better protector. Why dogs protect will be explained in a moment.

Biting and tugging games will only make your dog bite YOU. Play smart. Play active, not rough.

6. *Understand why dogs protect.* An awful ot of people think their dog will protect them better if they never let anyone else touch the dog, if they roughhouse and make the dog mean and aggressive, if they isolate the dog from all strangers, if they tease the dog and make him quick to anger. This way of raising a dog will make a nasty, biting dog, not a protective dog. Dogs protect their owners because they are pack animals and it is natural for them to protect their pack and their turf. Some dogs have more of this instinct than others, but even the gentlest dog may try to protect his owner when danger is real. (Do not try to test your dog by faking danger. It just won't work. He knows the genuine thing from the phony better than you or I.) A well-mannered, trained, playful, friendly dog *may* protect you when the chips are down. A vicious, nasty dog may do so, too. But the second dog is also likely to bite you, to bite inappropriately, to cause grief and damage in your very own family. Biting prevention makes sense for all dogs. So don't use excuses — he's too small, she's too cute, she'll outgrow it, I want him to protect the kids. And don't wait until you have to call in the Marines. Obedience training, teaching your dog limits, correcting all forms of aggression (including growling and nipping) and playing active but not rough should give you the dog you want. Remember, dogs aren't born bad. Given the right upbringing, any breed or mixed breed can be a solid, gentle, trustworthy canine citizen, a reliable pet and a loving companion.

6
Dog Training,
The Mini Series

SIT, STAY, come, down and heel in pictures and captions, step-by-step and very easy.

Mordecai Siegal

SIT

WHAT YOU WANT...

HOW TO GET IT...

1. Attract with toy   OR   2. Lift chin   OR   3. Pull up leash, push down rump

IF HE BREAKS _ANY_ COMMAND...

Say NO. Repeat command as you put him back where he was.

IF HE'S GOOD, BREAK HIM WITH "OKAY" AND PRAISE HIM...

STAY

WHAT YOU WANT...

HOW TO GET IT...

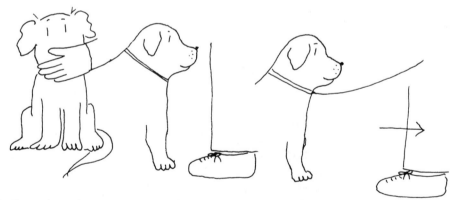

1. Give hand signal – swing hand slowly toward dog's face as you say "STAY."

2. Step in front of dog.

3. When dog is steady, back away to end of leash.

58

4. As your dog gets steadier, increase the distance and - - -

5. Add distractions!

COME

WHAT YOU WANT...

HOW TO GET IT...

1. Call your dog sweetly.

2. Praise when he comes.

3. Increase the distance. Tug, tug, tug if necessary.

4. Praise when he comes.

DOWN

WHAT YOU WANT...

DOWN

HOW TO GET IT...

NO

pat
pat

1. Pat floor and say "Down." Your dog will probably do nothing. So - - -

2. Pull his legs forward — gently.
   Proceed with caution. This command puts the dog in a submissive position, so it tends to get a lot of resistance. So - - -

3. When he's down, rub his belly to make him like lying down on command.

HEEL

WHAT YOU WANT...

HOW TO GET IT...

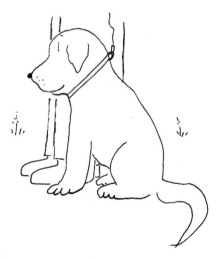

1. Start with your dog sitting squarely
   at your left side - - -

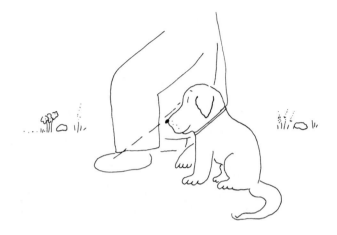

2. Say, "HEEL," and begin to walk, left leg first.

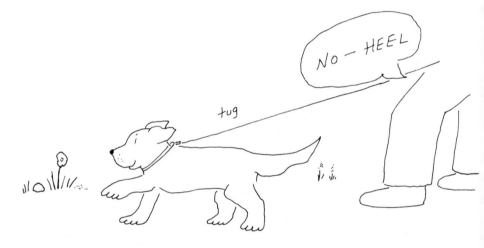

3. If he rushes ahead or lags behind, say, "NO -- HEEL," and tug him (once) back to your side. Praise and continue.

4. Whenever you stop, tell him to sit and praise him when he does.

5. Practice every day.

Mordecai Siegal

7

Dogs and Children, Safety First

In OUR HEARTS, we know that children and dogs are a natural combination. They are attracted to one another, both operating in a world of feelings, both living in the moment rather than in the past or the future, both knowing instinctively the value of cuddling, of trust, of unqualified love and friendship.

So how come so many kids get bitten by dogs? And, more importantly, how can this sorry state of affairs be corrected? Only one way. The kids need some education and so do the dogs.

Even if your kid doesn't have a dog, he should know when to touch a dog and when to let it be. A tied-up dog or a dog in a crate or dog pen should never be approached. A stray dog, a dog in a car, a loose dog in the park, these should not be handled. The only dogs a child (or adult) should pet are those he knows or those who are with their owner after the owner has given permission. Tied dogs, dogs in pens, dogs waiting outside of stores or in cars, these dogs may feel "on guard." They may be fine in their living rooms, but children should learn not to approach them in these circumstances. In addition, some dogs simply do not like children. Often this means that they were not exposed to children early on. They were improperly socialized. Children move more quickly and more erratically than do adults. They stumble more often and tend to make more noise, to shout suddenly. Their high pitched voices can absolutly unhinge some dogs, so all children should be taught not to scream or shriek around any dog. You can educate your kids without scaring them — simply make it clear, in a matter of fact, way, how to behave around dogs and which dogs can be handled and which dogs should be avoided. Happily, there are plenty of dogs around who adore children.

Children should learn how to approach even those friendly dogs. They should be told why each thing is so, because when you know *why*, you tend to remember. First, they should learn to approach a dog from the front, not the back. This is simply to avoid surprise and the possibility of startling a dog into a defensive mood. Children should be taught that dogs rely more on their noses than their eyes, so the dog should be offered the back of a loosely curled hand to smell. The curl is bigger than a flat hand and makes a less likely target for a bite, just in case. If the dog sniffs the hand and wags its tail, the child can pet the dog's head. If the dog's ears go back, he grins, he wags his tail more enthusiastically, he is inviting more and the child can then pet the dog's back. This gives both child and dog several stages of introduction and several clues about what is to come.

If any dog seems unreceptive to the hand, the child should quit right there. This is much safer than rushing up and grabbing at the dog or falling on him, which children sometimes do.

When you bring a dog home for your kids, both the kids and the dog need training. The dog needs to learn not to protect his food. He should be corrected and sent to his crate if he growls over his bowl or if he growls when someone enters the room when he's eating. This sort of behavior bodes ill, especially with young kids around. Your dog should allow you to remove his dish in the middle of his meal. Test this out cautiously by having your dog sit and stay, then adding another handful of dog food to the bowl. If this goes well, (try it with your dog on leash if you are unsure of him), in a few days, try again and remove the dish. Add some food. Praise as you immediately return dish to dog. Do not badger the dog, taking away every bite you give him to see if he'll object. Simply try him, leash on, once or twice. If he's good, praise him. If he growls, correct him with a strong NO and using the leash, march him away from the food and into his crate. Do not, under these circumstances, offer the food back to him until his next regularly scheduled mealtime.

Next be sure to monitor dogs and children. Young children can inadvertently hurt an animal, particularly a young or small animal. Children have to learn how to be gentle and this takes maturity and control. They need to learn, too, that dogs have the same sort of

70

feelings they do, that the doggy will get hurt if smacked with a toy or stepped on or if his hair or tail is pulled. They need to learn how to pet, carry and handle a dog, good advice that will last a lifetime. Puppies and dogs need to learn not to jump on children, not to grab toys and food from them, not to nip, growl or bite. So parents must keep an eye on kids and dogs to see that fun takes place in safety for both the child and the dog.

Should the dog sleep with your child? If the dog is gentle and reliable, sure — sometimes. A dog should never feel he has equal rights to any human bed. It gives him big ideas, alpha ideas. But there's nothing quite so comforting during a storm or while toughing out a virus as having your special dog curl up against your back or cuddle in your arms. Sure, let the dog sleep in your child's room and come up on the bed with permission. Make sure, teach him on your bed, he gets off when told OFF. If you must, use two people and use a leash to teach this lesson. One person should get into the bed. Call the dog up. Praise him. A few minutes later, point and tell the dog off. If he refuses to go, some will, have your partner tug the leash hard as you repeat the command OFF. Praise the dog once he's got four on the floor. However, if he continues to need to be tugged off the bed, rethink letting him up in the first place.

Make sure he gets off when told OFF!

What about responsibility for your dog?

I have always been against the notion of getting a child a pet so that the child will learn to be responsible. Children and dogs, that's about fun and companionship. Remember? Kindness toward another creature, the care-giving behavior we want our children to develop, thoughtfulness and gentleness, the ability to learn from observing and the wholesome contact with a natural creature, even that sense of responsibility, will probably happen. It shouldn't be forced.

Responsibility for pets should be in the mature and capable hands of adults. *You* should make sure the dog has fresh water and eats on time. You can always ask your kids to help — and then see that they do. But if you leave the care of a dog entirely up to young children, the dog may die of thirst! Sure, your kids are the greatest kids on earth, but they're still kids, aren't they? And that's precisely what they should be. Childhood is too short as it is. So for the child's sake and the dog's, keep *responsibility* the adult's, but have your children participate in the care of the dog with supervision. Remember the fun of being a kid and having a dog? Today's children need those kinds of memories, too.

Remember the fun of being a kid and having a dog?

8
What to Do When Problems Persist

YOU WERE full of hope and enthusiasm and feeling good about yourself. This time you didn't leave that stray Doberman with the sad eyes wandering in the park. You took her home. Or you adopted the nervous Shih Tzu when her owner died. (What could you do?) Or someone who knew you loved Great Danes tied one to your fence. At least, it was almost a Great Dane. So you sighed and put down another feed pan. Or when the kids said, "Please may we keep him, he followed us home," you said, "Sure, you can." Or when it was time to get a dog, you did the right thing, you went to the animal shelter and adopted one. Or when your best friend called and said you just *had* to see the two-year old Spaniel type her husband's cousin found on the side of the Thruway, like a jerk you went to see it. Now it's *still* marking your living room, six months later. Only now hope and enthusiasm and even the good feeling about yourself are all fading — as is your wall to wall. What now, dog lover?

The second-hand dog is second-hand for all his life. This is not to say he won't be a perfectly good pet. Some become the best of pets. But his history, like yours and mine, remains. And some of it may haunt him from time to time.

He's been disappointed. He put his love and trust in a person or in a family and they, perhaps because there was no other way and their hearts were broken over the matter, broke that trust. They gave him up. So while he may bond to you quickly, the memory is there. It's not a conscious thing. But someplace in the debris he's collected

73

"Please may I keep him, he followed me home."

as he's grown, a hurt remains. He may not adjust well to being left alone. The previously-owned dog is sometimes a chronic chewer who goes after the couch or toilet paper or fig plants every sixth or tenth time you go out without him. He may pace, cling, get underfoot. He's more likely to be unpredictable, too. And he's so big, that recycled Dane — how do you put him in a crate? And anyway, you did that six months ago. Should you do it still? Or is it too late? Too cruel? Not working?

And he's got fears you don't know the sources of. He won't walk past a flight of stairs. He runs when you turn the faucet on. He's afraid to walk through garage doors. He shakes a lot in his sleep.

And here you did this good thing. You took him in. So why is he still looking out the window now and then and crying? Why does he sometimes scan the street anxiously, checking every stanger, just in case? Doesn't he appreciate the effort you are making? Won't he ever change?

Dog problems, like most other problems, take more time to correct than you might imagine. No one ever promised you that being a saint would be easy, did they?

If your dog is still needy, give him more of what he needs.

1. He needs great expectations. He's lost that innocent anticipation of wonderful things in the wind. Give it back to him. Establish delicious routines that he can look forward to. Always take him with you for the mail — and teach him to carry it home. Always start the day with a little game before breakfast. Enlarge the routines of his care. Perhaps you could take a long walk with him before his meal. Follow his dinner with some grooming. If you work away from home, your homecoming could be magical (not hysterical — magical). Don't just unlock the door and say, "Hi." Start a conversation through the door. You speak. He speaks. You sneeze. He sneezes. And so on and so forth. Change your shoes and take him for a hike. Take a ball along. Later, at bedtime, give him a biscuit (buttered) to take to bed. Be predictable. Let him dream.

2. He needs exercise. He needs more exercise than most dogs because he's less secure than most dogs. If he's nervous or too thin, increase his food. Exercise will give him a better appetite. Controlled exercise — jogging, fast walking, biking with him, will help build him

Mordecai Siegal

Clean is good. Ask your mother.

up. And if it's warm out and there's a pond or a lake around, take him swimming. Water calms.

3. Bathe him at least once a month, but not more than once a week unless he meets a skunk. Use gentle dog shampoo. Once clean, he'll feel better and you'll want to handle him more. Clean is good. Ask your mother.

4. He needs friends. No matter how much you love each other, no matter how much time you spend with him, no matter how many cats, raccoons and gerbils you have, your dog needs the companionship of his own kind — dogs. (No, you are not his own kind.) He must get the chance to play with other dogs. You do not have to run out and get another, but do get him to the park or make dates with the nice dog down the block. In some way, he must be allowed that which he can get nowhere else — communication and interaction with his own species.

5. He needs to be socialized. Of course I repeat myself! But think about this — how long did he sit in that kennel or shelter? How long did he wander around, filthy and unloved? To make sure he's socialized, do the job again — and again. Take him everywhere. Pretend he's your Siamese twin. Make history. Be the first in your neighborhood to take your dog out of the yard. Start a precedent with your pre-owned, beautifully-mannered, magnificently-trained, terrific, needy pet. (He's not trained? Kindly send me your name and address and one of my representatives will make you an offer you can't refuse.)

6. You trained him, right? Since you've done the basics (they are right in this book — and pretty easy to teach), go on to higher education. If he's sound, teach him to jump. Two cinder blocks and an old broomstick will do. You don't want him to leap tall buildings in a single bound. He might then start jumping fences. Has he got a nose? Teach him scent games — find the cookie or find the ball. He'll love it. Take him to dog school. It's fun and social and you'll both learn a lot. He's a smart cookie. Let him use his brain.

7. Teach him to stay alone — without hysterics. Let us not forget that there is another side to all this attention your dog is getting. He's

Teach him to stay alone — without hysterics.

got to come to terms with your right to come and go. He's got to become trustworthy when you are not home. A crate is a tool. It's not forever. This means you have to take some chances. So — when it's the couch he goes after as you are pulling out of the driveway, keep him crated. When he gets his anxiety level down enough to merely eat the leaves off a poor fig plant, take a chance. Of course, you'll make sure the poisonous plants are out of reach or, better still, off to live with someone who has no pets. Exercise him. Brush him. Give him a boiled bone or some rawhide. Leave the radio on. And make your outings short and matter of fact the first dozen times or so he's got run of the house. Don't be hysterical when you come home. And try to work it out with him. It's nice if you can leave home once in a while. After all, people have needs, too.

8. Take inventory. When you're feeling blue and thinking he'll never improve, take inventory. Think about how he was — and how things are now. Sure, he still slips back now and then. Who's perfect? But he's put on twelve pounds and his coat has thickened up. And he wags his tail a lot more now. And he sits and comes and lies down and even stays for a few minutes before he starts whining. And when you say GO HOME, GO HOME, he knows exactly where to run. He no longer gets carsick, usually. He's stopped growling at the dog next door. So what if you still have to crate him now and then or if he chews an occasional plant. When you stop to think how far he's come, it will give you the energy to continue.

Tighten his training and add something new each month or so — a trick, a game, a new command, a new level of an old command. Keep him well-fed, clean and exercised. Talk to him. But give him quiet time, too. Let him think his own thoughts, whatever they may be. And when his dreams of rabbit chasing and unlimited burgers are interrupted from time to time by dim, frightening memories of the desert his life was before he found you, let him be. There are parts of other lives we cannot touch. You do your part. You leave the rest alone.

Need more help? Read on. The training secrets professional trainers use follow.

"The Dog You'd Like to Have . . . "

9
Professional Secrets You Can Use

CAN YOU USE a professional trainer's secret methods to elevate the level of your training, to be happier as you work, to become more efficient, faster, more successful in reaching your goal, a terrific, well-trained, second-hand dog? Why not? Here they are:

1. Always set long-term goals. Think ahead to the dog you'd like to have: obedient off-leash on voice and/or hand signals, calm when company comes, does a few dignified tricks, jogs with you and doesn't run off to chase rabbits in the middle of your run, doesn't steal food or dig on the couch. Plan how you're going to get there. Plan all the little steps that will help you have the dog you want. Don't do anything in early training that will spoil it for your larger goal.

2. Always set short-term goals. These goals are for each lesson. For example, Monday's goal is to get that automatic sit on the heel. You do go over other work. But your main focus is in achieving the automatic sit and, once you get *one*, you praise the dog to the sky and end the session with a game. Tuesday's goal is to speed up the recall. You warm the dog up with some fast heeling and a few quick sit-stays and down-stays. Then you use every trick in the book to speed the recall. You call him and run backwards. You play recall games, calling him back and forth between two of his favorite people. You praise a lot. You forego the automatic sit in favor of speed, for a while. You break away from him, yelling out COME, COME, COME. When he runs straight to you, you praise and quit for the day. And so forth.

3. Use a daily lesson plan. Jot down what your dog does well, badly, not at all. And jot down your goals, long-term and short. Then make a couple of brief notes after each session on what you achieved and what you wish to achieve next time. It helps a lot.

4. Stick to one problem during each lesson. You can review all your old work, but, basically, deal with one problem at a time: a crooked sit, naughty jumping up, forging ahead or whatever else needs your attention.

5. Pretend he's not yours. When you get into touble because he's sooo cute and you "wuv" him soooo much, pretend he's not yours. Pretend you *are* a professional trainer, working for money and you've *got* to get this little darling trained or you don't eat! We're all blind with our own pets. Yet we can see clearly what's wrong with other people's dogs (and kids). So, while you work, detach yourself from ownership of your dog. You'll be surprised how clear-eyed you get. (When I have a problem with my dogs, Scarlet or Lefty, I panic. Then I remember to pretend that someone has called me and described this very dog, this very problem and it's shocking how smart I suddenly get when the dog "isn't mine.")

6. Follow work with play. Some owners are more serious than most trainers. Work well and efficiently. Save the last few minutes for a goofy game. It's the best reward for trainer and dog.

7. Work a tired dog. If your exuberant, huge, young, strong dog is just too much for you, you are probably working him without exercising him. Ideally (long-term goal), he should work well no matter what. But to start (short-term goal), give him a run for his money and *then* get him to heel. It's a stroke of genius. You'll see.

8. Use the best equipment money can buy. Don't expect to go out there and break your hand on a chain or burn it on a nylon lead and then love training your dog. Get a good leather or cotton canvas leash. If you don't let him chew it, it will last a lifetime. And get a good collar, too, appropriate to the size and type of dog you have.

82

Carol Lea Benjamin

(Don't assume you need a choke chain for all dogs. A leather collar is fine for many.)

9. Reward yourself for work well done. Of course you reward your dog. You pet him, praise him, play with him. But if you work like a pro, *you* need a reward, too. Think of something that will help you motivate yourself and, by gosh, do it.

10. Always take the time to be alpha. No trainer worthy of the name would touch a dog without establishing alpha status. Of course, when you train professionally, being alpha is a *fait accompli.* You live it and you breathe it every day. With your own pet, this should be so, too. But, just in case, take the time to prove it. A long down will do. A long sit-stay will do it. A firm voice helps. Good, solid, appropriate eye contact is a must. Then, and only then, take the leash and do your session.

11. Don't forget eye contact as you work. It is the language of canines. It is not just a "trick" to become alpha, it is the meat and potatoes of communicating with dogs. Your eyes can actually transmit approval and disapproval to your dog. They can project love, too. Practice what I preach. Transmit and receive via the eye.

12. Be humble. Each new day, your dog will teach *you* something new, if you let him. Keep your eye out for interesting reactions. Find out, by looking, what he thinks, how he learns, how he tries to get away with things. If you ever think you know it all, you'll stop growing. Instead, practice humility and let the beasts teach you. You'll love it.

13. Never be afraid to be creative. Invent, calculate, innovate! When one method doesn't work, try another, then another, until you find out what gets through to this particular dog. When you are stuck, keep reading, keep trying. If you work in a fair, humane, firm, loving way, like your dog's mother, you will never go astray. Nor do you have to stick with the tried and true. After all, *your* methods may be the tried and true one day.

Professional trainers know that there's always something more to learn about dogs, that exciting new concepts and methods are always around the corner. If you work like a professional, using the secrets

84

professional trainers use, you will not only be quicker and better at your task, you will be more receptive to learning, more content in the work, more appreciative of the learner. Those, friends, are worthy goals.

Mordecai Siegal

10

Practice, Practice (to keep training tight and the relationship right)

E VERY DOG'S TRAINING slips and slides when it's neglected. The long down may be rusty. The come might be slow. The automatic sit might need a reminder every now and then. The stand may get you a *who, me?* It's only natural for training to deteriorate if it is not being used. So when you find your dog suffering from intermittent deafness, don't rush out and get him a hearing aid — practice, paractice. He'll never get to Carnegie Hall if you don't.

When I see my dog's training looking shabby, I push. I remind her that I'm alpha. I do a little tune-up every day for at least a week. I sit under a tree and reflect upon what I've been doing — and not doing. And I practice what I preach, requiring sharp, zestful, snappy work when the curriculum calls for obedience and fire and wit in her lovely eyes when it calls for play. You recall — all work and no play, etc. Do as I do. Here's how:

1. Push, push. It's canine. When a dog wants to tell the pack (canine or human) that he's alpha, he pushes — literally. He leans, he shoves, he hogs the bed, he walks down the middle of the sidewalk. Lean back. When you heel your dog, veer off to the left. Make him

Make him sit while you fix his dinner.

Be careful. He might hear you!

watch out for you. Push gently with your ankle, calf or thigh (depending upon the size of the dog in question) and get those feet moving, get those eyes watching you, get some respect. Push, too, in the figurative sense. He does. Does he break a stay after three minutes? Go for twenty. (Sure he can!) Does he meander in on the come? Do ten in a row, on leash, running backwards — and get that sit front, too. Is it all your fault? Have you been sloppy, friend? Who cares! Guilt isn't productive. Work is. So, push. Shove. Tighten it up.

2. Remind the dog that you're alpha. Again. Try the long, long down. He *can* do an hour. So what if you have to put him back down a few times. That's part of the work of being alpha, isn't it? Try eye contact. Tell him to look at you and see that he does. Now you can praise him. When you're out in the park, get those eyes now and then. When he's heeling, click, click with your tongue. When he looks at you, praise. When he's eating, tell him NO and take away his food. (Do this no more than once a week unless you like stitches.) That's alpha. Alpha means boss. It means number one. It means privilege. That's you, babe, privileged. And don't you forget it — or he will.

3. Do a Spring tune-up. I train my dog all the time. Oh, she's not perfect. Far from it. But if I let a week or two go by without a ten-minute lesson here or there, she elects herself president. She's assertive. That's just how she is. She keeps me on my toes.

Your dog may appear to be submissive. He may take that route to the top. Is his training sloppy? That's his message. Tough or stubborn or what have you, give a few commands and judge for yourself. Chances are your dog can use a little tune-up, too. In fact, even if he doesn't, it couldn't hurt to make a habit of it. Make part of some of his outings lesson time. Try out each command. Check out the automatic sit. Is it indeed still automatic? Is it quick and straight and executed with equanimity? No one I know needs a resentful automatic sit! Do that long down. Does he stay — the whole time? Make him sit while you fix his dinner, just the way you did when he was a puppy. And make him wait for the OKAY before he pigs out. Don't forget. *Rules and regulations make a dog feel secure.* Now you're cooking. Good for you.

While you're at it, while your focus is on your dog, how about a little Spring cleaning, too? While he's in the tub, teach him TURN AROUND so you can get both sides clean. And if he has the habit of shaking as soon as you get him wet and again as soon as he's full of soap, just watch his head. It will move first. If when he starts to move his head, you put a gentle hand on his muzzle to stop him, he won't shake and you won't get soaked. Until later.

Check his ears, too. You can clean them with a wash cloth. Maybe he really can't hear you! Check his feet and pads. Let him know you're on top of *everything*.

4. Think it over. Why has his training slipped? The answer is there *somewhere*. Has he started sleeping in your bed and does he thus feel equal — or superior — to you? Do you just not bother to reinforce what you ask him to do? I have heard — so many times — "Arnold, COME. Okay, Arnold, don't come." Be careful. He might hear you! What are you doing that is encouraging a sloppy response to training? Find out. Fix it.

5. Practice what I preach. When you take your dog out to work him, take him out. Go away from home. Take him to the main drag. Take him to the distractions. Now watch him. This is not your time for window shopping or shop talk. Keeping your eyes on your dog, get some sharp responses. Go for speed. Go for snappy, happy responses. If you're not getting them, there's a reason — and it's not his age or breed. Of course a Collie doesn't work like a Basset Hound and amen to that. But the Collie, the Basset, the mixed breed, whatever, can work faster and better as himself than what he is probably doing now. He can improve. Who couldn't? And you can help him to do so.

Give your dog energy as you work and give him the benefit of your high expectations. Know he can do it and help him prove you right. Praise him like crazy when you've pushed and gotten what you were after. Ah. Good. Now let's go home and play a game.

6. All work and no play makes for a stiff relationship with a dog. Do you dress up as a tiger to amuse your children or spouse? Do you keep waking your children up to say good-night again? Do you make a fool of yourself just to get your spouse or friend or aging parent to

90

Maybe your dog can teach you how to be silly again.

Benjamin 1987

laugh? Why not? Maybe your dog can teach you how to be silly again — just like when you were a silly kid and didn't care who knew it.

Me, I laugh at my dog's jokes, even the dumb ones. In that way, I encourage her to play more jokes on me, to be silly, stupid and fun. In turn, I am silly, stupid and fun, too.

My dogs and I race through the house trying to beat each other to some chosen spot. We sneak up on each other — and then we sneak up on my husband, Steve. I hide and let the dogs find me. I hide things and encourage the dogs to find the things. Sometimes Scarlet, my Shepherd, "hides" from me, usually by going somewhere she's not allowed like the bed and then she grins and beats her tail in fake submission when I find her there. (If it were real submission, why would she be up there in the first place?) Sometimes to get my dogs to play with me I act like a dog. I pant and crawl, I shove and push. I roll around on the floor. I play bow and they bow back. I'm a complete fool. You know you can be one, too. It's neat.

We play games out of doors, too. Scarlet and Lefty, the Shiba, like to jump over low fences in the park. They like to walk on benches and barriers. These things build confidence and add agility. Scarlet loves to carry a stick, the bigger the better, when she's out hiking. Lefty loves to chase leaves, bits of paper, anything that blows in the wind. A dog can't heel all the time can he?

What does your dog love to do? Can you invent a game for him that incorporates his favorite activities — retrieving, running, swimming, chasing, carrying a ball. toy or stick, carrying your groceries in a backpack, jumping over obstacles, climbing under or over things, digging a hole, whatever? The game need not look like a game to anyone but you and your dog. What's fun and what's funny can be a very personal thing.

When work or fun have slipped away, practice, practice. The dog is forgiving. He'll be back where he belongs in no time.

Stephen Lennard

About the Author

CAROL LEA BENJAMIN, a professional dog trainer, has written many books about dogs and other subjects for both adults and children, including DOG TRAINING FOR KIDS, CARTOONING FOR KIDS, WRITING FOR KIDS, RUNNING BASICS, DOG PROBLEMS, DOG TRICKS, MOTHER KNOWS BEST; THE NATURAL WAY TO TRAIN YOUR DOG and two novels, THE WICKED STEPDOG and NOBODY'S BABY NOW.

As a dog writer, Carol Benjamin is regarded very highly. In 1985 she was named WRITER OF THE YEAR by The Dog Writers' Association of America and in that same year she was voted DOGDOM'S WRITER OF THE YEAR, making her a winner of the prestigious FIDO AWARD.

Her children's books have twice received starred reviews in *The School Library Journal*, have twice been selected among Children's Books of the Year by Bank Street College and have been well reviewed widely, including in *The New York Times*, *The Los Angeles Times*, *Saturday Review* and *Newsweek*.

Ms. Benjamin's articles about dogs and other subjects have appeared in *Time*, *Better Homes and Gardens*, *Medical Economics*, *Private Practice*, *Apartment Life*, *Off-Lead*, *Runners' World*, *The German Shepherd Dog Review*, *Animals* and many others. She is an international advisor to DOGS U*S*A* and writes a monthly column, DOG TRAINER'S DIARY, for *Pure-Bred Dogs/American Kennel Gazette*, the official publication of THE AMERICAN KENNEL CLUB. She has also had numerous appearances on radio, television and for kennel clubs as an expert on dog behavior.

Ms. Benjamin is a member of The Authors' Guild and The Dog Writers' Association of America.

Carol Benjamin lives in Greenwich Village with her husband, architect Stephen Lennard, and their dogs, the beautiful Scarlet, a German Shepherd and Lefty, a charming, second-hand Japanese Shiba Inu.